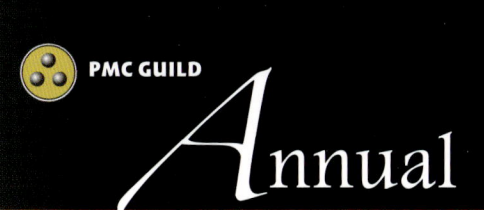

PMC GUILD

Annual

#1

Special thanks to the jurors;
 Jeanette Landenwitch
 Hattie Sanderson
 Robert Dancik
 Hadar Jacobson

Front cover: Jill Rockwell
Back Cover (clockwise)
 Hattie Sanderson
 Catherine Davies-Paetz
 Holly Gage
 Lise Moody

For ordering and permissions please contact
Director@PMCguild.com

ISBN 1-929565-25-9

Printed in Hong Kong

Introduction

This is the first edition of what will be an annual showcase of exceptional work in PMC. Artists from around the world were invited to submit photos of their work, which was then reviewed and assessed by a panel of four artists who are respected professionals in the PMC community. Each year a different panel of jurors will be selected.

In jurying the images, the qualities and elements looked for were:
- integral use of PMC
- quality of craftsmanship
- innovative design

The jury reviewed more than 1000 images, and in the end selected the 56 artists whose work we see here. The Guild wants to thank our four jurors for their dedicated (and volunteer) work in making this book a reality. Thanks also to all the artists who submitted work. Enjoy this book; look through it often, but then get back to work— before you know it, we'll be seeking work for next year's Annual.

Jurors' Statements

Jeanette Landenwitch
(Jury Chairperson)
"I was particularly pleased to see a great diversity of work. The obvious talent made the choices difficult. Congratulations to those whose work was chosen. The PMC community is alive and well! Keep on creating!"

Hattie Sanderson
"Submissions for the premier publication of the *PMC Guild Annual* included an overwhelming number of superbly crafted metal clay pieces from a large pool of very talented artists. It has been an honor and a privilege to be a juror for this publication, yet a difficult task to choose the top submissions. Congratulations to those whose work was chosen for the book. The continuing evolution of the medium is very evident in this body of work. May it inspire us all."

Hadar Jacobson
"While at first it seemed to me unfair to judge a work of art based on an image only, it made sense when I remembered that the work is juried for a publication, not an art show, and that the photo should be as good as the work. I suspect that a lot of the photography was not doing justice to the photographed piece, and regret that some wonderful artists did not make their way into this publication."

Robert Dancik
"The talent, creativity, and resourcefulness of the artists using PMC is always amazing and inspiring, and the work submitted for jurying is a testimony to this. It was my good fortune and delight to be able to view each piece of work, and an honor to be part of this first annual publication. Congratulations are in order to everyone involved with this endeavor."

Evan J. Soldinger

Linda Kaye-Moses

Shirinszhar
Fine silver, sterling, 18k gold,
spessartite on quartz, tourmaline
3¼" by 1½"

Robert Diamante

Celie Fago

Pod Pendant
Fine silver, 24k keum-boo
3" tall

Stephanie Frymyer

Stephanie Frymyer

The Angel Within
Fine silver, abalone shell
2½" by 2"

Stephanie Frymyer

Stephanie Frymyer

The Angel Within
Fine silver, abalone shell
2½" by 2"

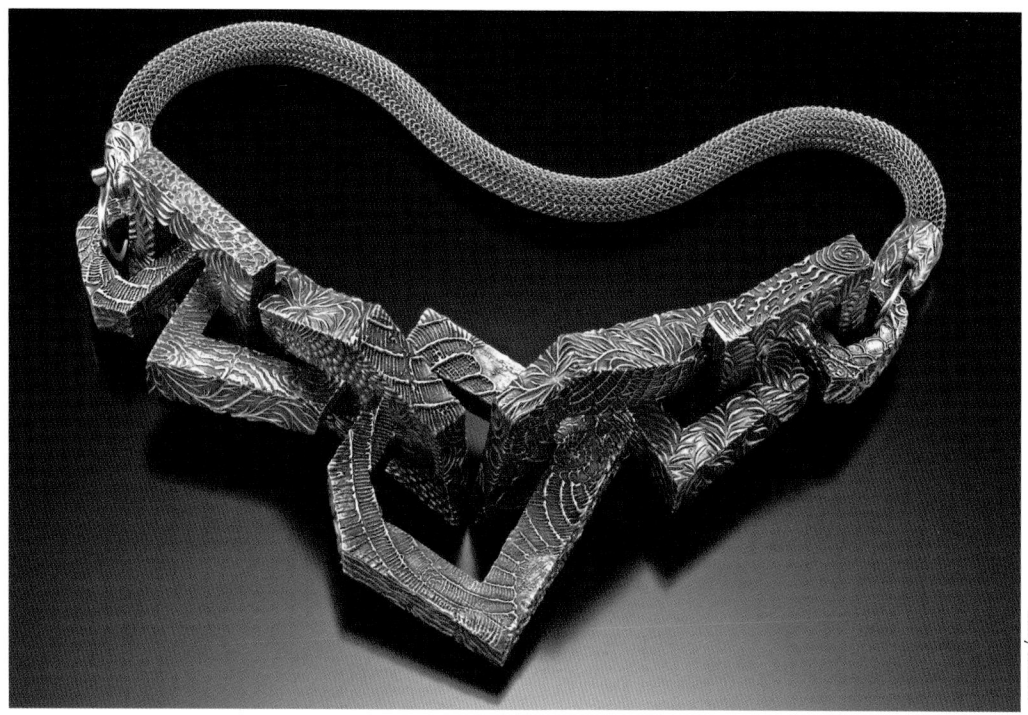

Larry Sanders

Barbara Becker Simon

Big Links
Fine silver

Lise Moody

Hell's Broomstick (brooch)
Fine silver, sterling
4" long

Jeanette Landenwitch

Jeanette Landenwitch

Black Onyx Necklace
Fine silver, black onyx
18" long

Terry Long

Julie G. Mazakas

Ceremonial Wine Cup
Fine silver
4½"

Catherine Davies-Paetz

Catherine Davies-Paetz

Sea Dreams
Fine silver, sterling, 24k gold
3¼" by 2"

A. Baduel-Crispin

Angela Baduel-Crispin

Where's Paradise (ring)
Fine silver, soft drink pull tab,
plastic grass, polymer clay
2½" tall

Hadar Jacobson

Toni Ellis

Dragon Village Tea Set
Fine silver
2½" tall

Frank Poole

Nancy Karpel

Wisdom (brooch)
Fine silver, gold, garnet,
pearl, tourmaline.
3" tall

Richard Brunck

Debbie Clifford

Malachite Glasswing (earrings)
Fine silver, plique-a-jour enamel
1¾" tall

Hadar Jacobson

Hadar Jacobson

The Wall (necklace)
Fine silver, moonstone,
semipreious beads
4" tall

Robert Diamante

Tim McCreight

Sumi brush
Fine silver, linen, goat hair
6" long

Robert Diamante

Tim McCreight

Sumi brush
Fine silver, wood, straw, linen,
goat hair
6" long

Holly Gage

Holly Gage

Winter Dance
Fine silver, cubic zirconia, dandrite
1½" tall

Larry Sanders

Barbara Becker Simon

Marathon Beads
Fine silver, 22k gold

Sara Krempel

Sara Krempel

Breakthrough (pendant)
Fine silver, shakudo, hematite
3" tall

Bruce Shippee

Nancy Hamilton

Beauty
Fine silver, 22k gold, sterling, pearls,
apatite, sapphire, blue diamonds
2½" tall

Robert Diamante

Jennifer Kahn

Reversible Shell Pendant
Fine silver, shell
1¼" diameter

Corrin Jacobsen Kovalcik

Terry Kovalcik

Crane Pendant
Fine silver, 22k gold
1³/₈" tall

Naoko Tanaka

Jyomon
Fine silver, quartz crystal
2" tall

A. Lingener-Reece

Anne Lingener-Reece

Untitled necklace
Fine silver, 24k gold, boulder opal,
pink tourmaline, shells,
aquamarine beads
6" tall

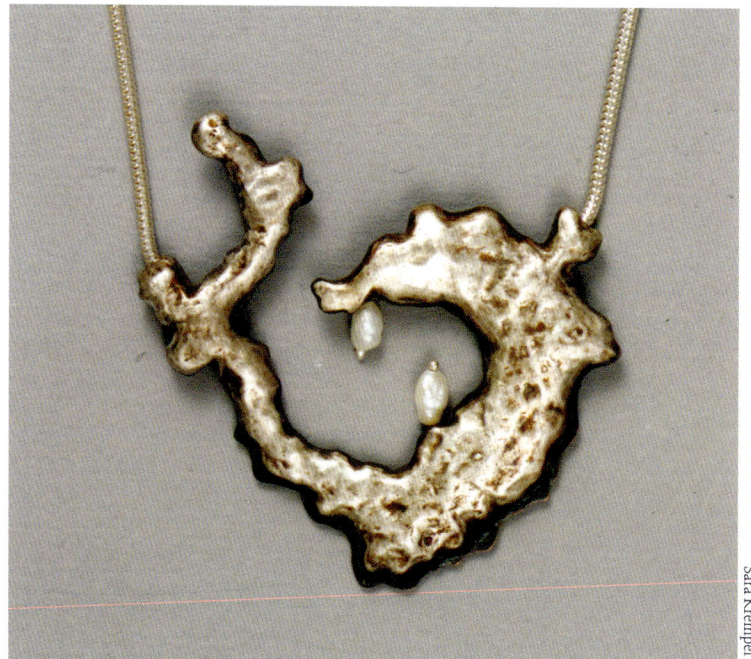

Sara Krempel

Sara Krempel

Wandering (pendant)
Fine silver, shakudo, pearls
1¾" tall

Lynda McCann-Olson

Pendant
Fine silver, enamel

F'ap Sakwa

Shahasp Valentine

Knife Edge Necklace #17
Fine silver, 24k gold, diamond, pearl
2¼" tall

Hap Sakwa

Shahasp Valentine

Knife Edge Necklace #14
Fine silver, 24k gold,
sapphire, pearls
2" tall

Barbara Briggs

Barbara Briggs

Elements II (bracelet)
Fine silver
7½" long

Barbara Briggs

Barbara Briggs

Charmed (necklace)
Fine silver
22" long

Tami Meader

Robyn A. Krutch

The Bees Feast
Fine silver, 22k gold, freshwater pearls,
pigmented Milestone
largest form is 2¾" diameter

Hadar Jacobson

Laurie Edelman

Peeping People
Fine silver
3" tall

Holly Gage

Holly Gage

Large Pod Necklace
Fine silver, freshwater pearls
Pods are 3"

Catherine Witherell

Jointed Bird Pendants
Fine silver, sterling
1 ¾" tall

Laurie Latham

Lora Hart

Waters of Life (vessel)
Fine silver
1 3/8" tall

Hadar Jacobson

Hadar Jacobson

11 Rocks (necklace)
Fine silver
16" long

A. Lingener-Reece

Anne Lingener-Reece

Just Dessert (bowl & spoon)
Fine silver, enamel
2" tall by 5½" wide

Tami Meader

Robyn A. Krutch

Aesop's Crow (pendant)
Fine silver, beach glass
3½" tall

Hattie Sanderson

Mardi Gras
Fine silver, dichoric glass, freshwater pearl,
faux drusy, found objects
3¼" wide

Hadar Jacobson

Toni Ellis

Teknobat
Fine silver, sterling,
glass beads
3½" high

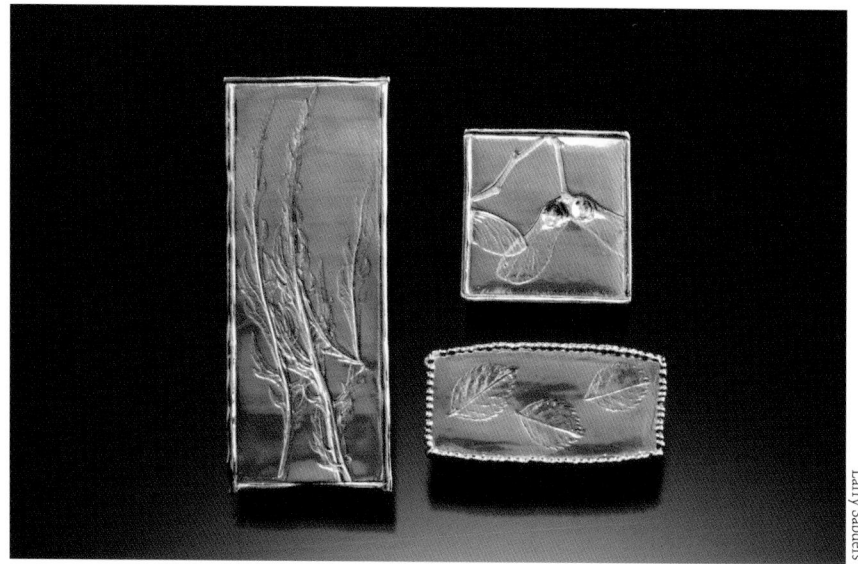

Larry Sabders

Susan Northrup

Square
Fine silver
largest: 2½" tall

Image Construction Studio

Nancy Karpel

Mayan Ruin Pin
Fine silver, 24k & 18k gold,
sterling, sapphires,
fossilized sand dollar
3" tall

Robert Diamante

Jennifer Kahn

Large Turquoise Necklace
Fine silver, turquoise

Corrin Jacobsen Kolvalcik

Terry Kovalcik

Inca
Fine silver, sterling
1 3/16" wide

Jeanette Landenwitch

Jeanette Landenwitch

Tree of Life Celtic Vessel
Fine silver, enamel
2⁷/₈" tall

A. Lingener-Reece

Anne Lingener-Reece

Untitled pendant
24k, platinum, white and yellow
diamonds, black cultured pearl
2" by 2"

Hadar Jacobson

Hadar Jacobson

Ocean Houses (necklace)
Fine silver, Mexican fire opals
2¼" wide each

Larry Sanders

Barbara Becker Simon

Big Rings
Fine silver, 22k gold,
cubic zirconia

Robert Diamante

Barbara Becker Simon

Tautology
Fine silver, sterling, Effetre,
sodalime, & dichroic glass,
bead diameters are ¾"

Keiko Narazaki

Keiko Narazaki

Untitled ring
Fine silver

C. Davies-Paetz

Catherine Davies-Paetz

New Metal, Ancient Vision
Fine silver, sterling, 24k
1 $\frac{5}{8}$" tall

Evan Soldinger

Linda Kaye-Moses

In a Pale Garden
Fine silver, sterling, 14k, fossilized coral,
rose quartz, mother of pearl
4½" tall

Image Construction Studio

Nancy Karpel

Cenate (pendant)
Fine silver, 14, 18 & 24k gold,
sterling, sapphires, opal,
tourmalinated quartz, enamel
3" tall

Robert Diamante

Celie Fago

Bird Box Ring
Fine silver, 24k gold keum-boo,
18k gold, sterling
Box is ¾" diameter

Susan McManus

Mark Lattanzi

Tidepool Bracelet
Fine silver, sterling, 22k gold,
topaz, rainbow moonstones
7" long

Yukiko Tsuda

Necklace
Fine silver, gemstones

Drew Davidson

Tonya Davidson

Geisha's Gold
Fine silver, 24k gold, pearl, resin

Robert Diamante

Celie Fago

Hinged box
Fine silver, 18k gold
1½" square

Jill Rockwell

Necklace
Fine silver, sterling,
semi-precious stones

Lisa Cain

Rocket Moon (brooch)
Fine silver, sapphire

Hattie Sanderson

Hattie Sanderson

Large Pearl Ring
Fine silver, fine gold,
freshwater pearl

Hattie Sanderson

Hattie Sanderson

Mabe Pearl Ring
Fine silver, fine gold,
Mabe pearl

Scott Taylor Photography

Janet Harriman

Collage (pendant)
Fine silver, enamel
1¼" tall

Deena Love

Fish 2 (pendant)
Fine silver, acrylic paint, grass,
stones, epoxy resin
1½" by 2"

Akiko Nakaya

Akiko Nakaya

Inner Space (bracelet)
Fine silver
6" diameter

Barbara Briggs

Barbara Briggs

Stoned (necklace)
Fine silver, sterling, 24k gold,
18k/silver bi-metal, granite
16" long

Catherine Witherell

Catherine Witherell

Birdhouse (pendant)
Fine silver, sterling,
freshwater pearls, tourmaline
house is 1 1/8" tall

Bruce Shippee

Nancy Hamilton

Space Flower
Fine silver, sterling, amethyst,
tourmaline
5" tall

Fred Baker

Cheryl Baker

Peacock Nest
Fine silver, sterling, dichroic glass
1 1/8" diameter

Colleen Stella

Colleen Stella

Moon River
Fine silver, enamel
1¾" tall

Mary Ann Devos

Mask (fibula)
Fine silver, copper, brass,
ceramic beads

Linda Warner

Linda Warner

Untitled pendant
Fine silver, sterling,
Rocky Butte jasper
2" tall

C. Davies-Paetz

Catherine Davies-Paetz

Silver Runs Through It (brooch)
Fine silver, sterling, 24k gold
2⁵/₈" long

Karen Blough

Sara Jayne Cole

Daffodil I
Fine silver

Jean Hayes

Jean Hayes

Untitled neckpiece
Fine silver, cubic zirconias

Robert Diamante

Tim McCreight

Untitled brooch
Fine silver, glass
3½" wide

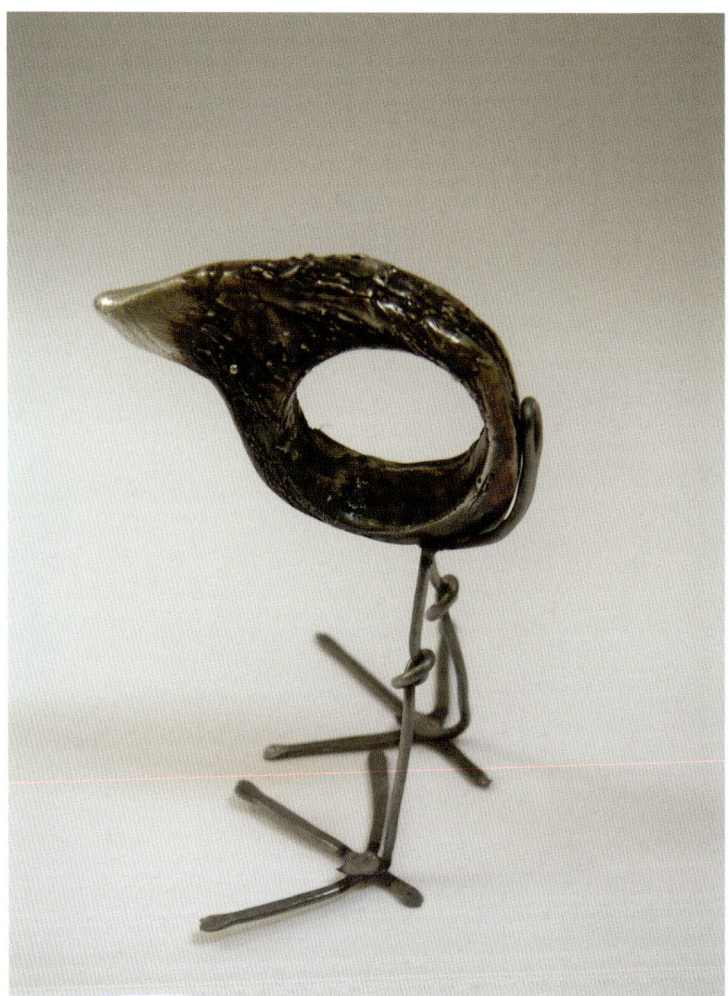

Rebecca Skeels

Hairy (ring in stand)
Fine silver, mild steel

Deb Steele

Tree Trio with Gold
Fine silver, 22k gold
2" tall

Linda Warner

Linda Warner

Untitled pendant
Fine silver, sterling,
Mexican crazy lace agate
1½" tall

Joseph Ward

Marian Ward

Untitled Bracelet
Fine silver, garnet,
moonstone, 24k gold
6" by 2"

Keiko Narazaki

Keiko Narazaki

Untitled ring
Fine silver

Suguru Bakoshi

Fish (pendant)
Fine silver

Hadar Jacobson

Toni Ellis

Agamemnon (bracelet)
Fine silver
7⁵/₈" by 1¼"

Drew Davidson

Tonya Davidson

Ripples in Time (brooch)
Fine silver, 18k gold, pearl

William Gallagher

Angela Gallagher

Treasure from Trash (fibula)
Fine silver, sterling
3½" tall

Holly Gage

Holly Gage

Small Pods (necklace)
Fine silver, cubic zirconia,
freshwater pearls
16" long

Rosey Boehm

Roz Eberhard

Caught by the Breeze (neckpiece)
Fine silver; 22k gold

Diane Madu

Julie Keating

Small Vessels
Fine silver, ceramic,
turquoise, glass

Nancy Hamilton

Nancy Hamilton

Thistle
Fine silver, cubic zirconia
4" tall

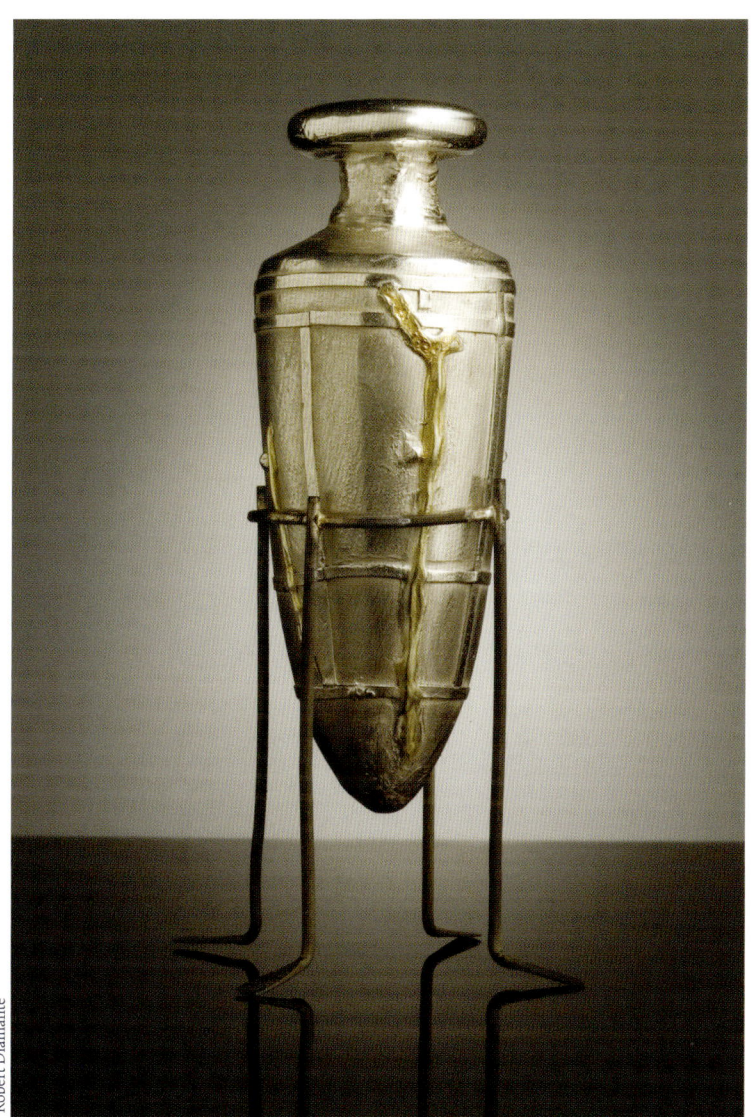

Robert Diamante

Tim McCreight

Small Vessel
fine silver, 22k gold,
steel stand
3" tall

Evan Soldinger

Linda Kaye-Moses

Meikyu (ring)
Fine silver, 24k gold

Jeanette Landenwitch

Jeanette Landenwitch

Briny Sea Necklace
Fine silver, sterling,
enamel, flourite beads
18" long

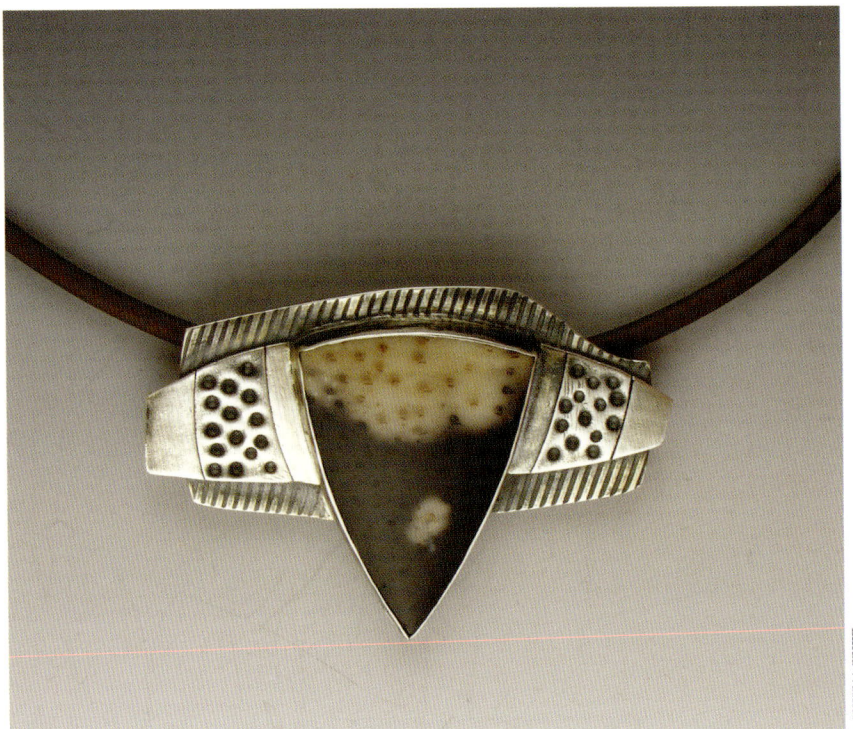

Linda Warner

Linda Warner

Untitled pendant
Fine silver, rubber,
petrified palmwood
1¾" by 2½"

Linda Warner

Linda Warner

Untitled pendant
Fine silver, sterling, moss agate
1½" by 2¾"

Donna Penoyer

Donna Penoyer

Mamma, Did You Sing?
(whistling ring)
Fine silver, blue spinel
1¾" tall

Stephanie Frymyer

Stephanie Frymyer

Abstract Beauty (ring)
Fine silver, freshwater pearls,
synthetic aquamarine

Nancy Karpel

Nancy Karpel

Folded Shell (brooch)
Fine silver, sterling, 14k gold, garnet
2½" tall

Hadar Jacobson

Toni Ellis

Bela
Fine silver, sterling,
garnets
2"

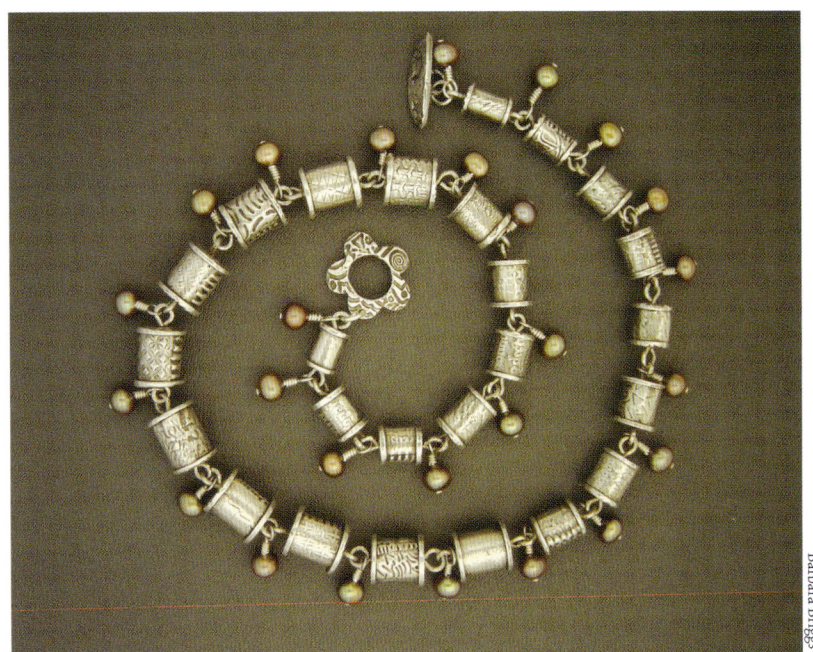

Barbara Briggs

Barbara Briggs

Cylinders (necklace)
Fine silver, freshwater pearls
17" long

Mary Ann Devos

Bird Nest
Fine silver

A. Basuel-Crispin

Angela Baduel-Crispin

OM Prayer Wheel
Fine silver, sterling, Faux Bone,
24k & 22k gold, brass, ebony,
natural bone, hematite

C. Jacobsen-Kovalcik

Terry Kovalcik

Gone Fishin'
Fine silver, sterling, copper
1¾" tall

C. Davies-Paetz

Catherine Davies-Paetz

All Lined Up
Fine silver; 24k gold
1¼" tall by 1¾" wide

Patrik Kusek

Botanical Bracelet
Fine silver
7½" long

Donna Penoyer

Fish Man Whistle
Fine silver
2¼" tall

Jan Carpenter

Jan Carpenter

Mush–Mansion
Fine silver, sterling,
magnet clasp
1 5/8" by 5/8"

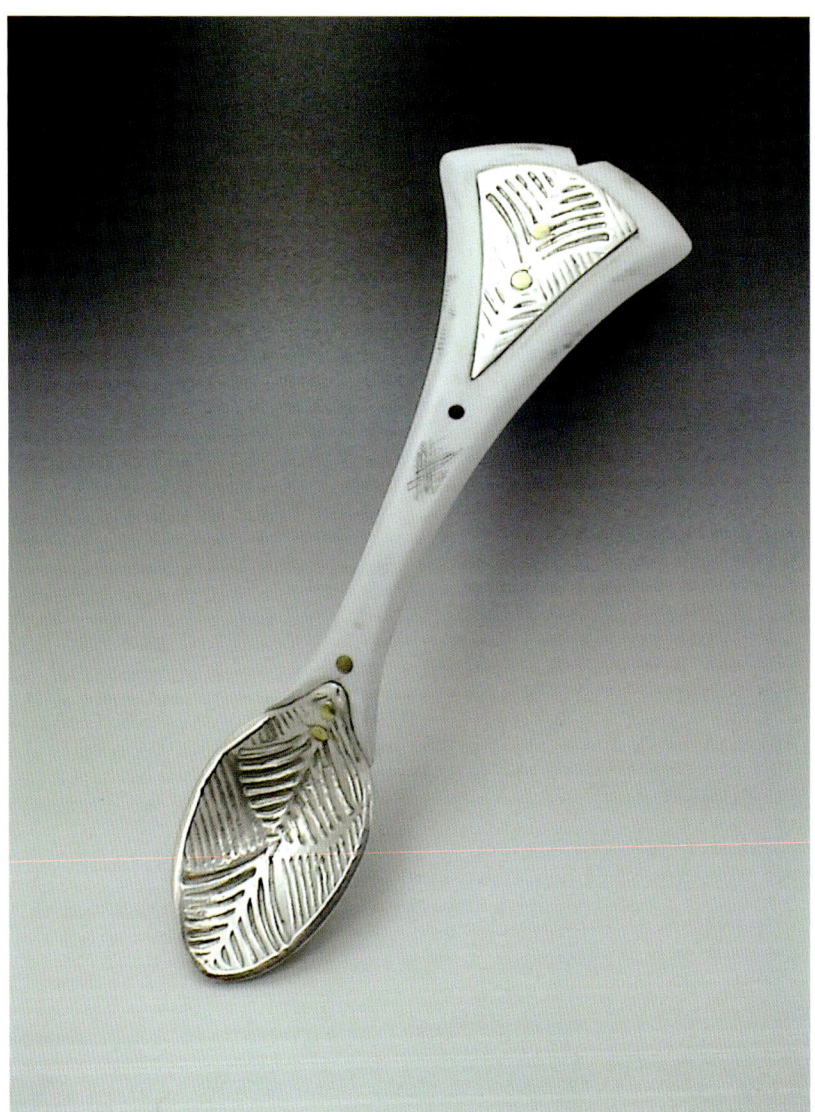

A. Baduel-Crispin

Angela Baduel-Crispin

Born With an Urban-Ethnic Spoon in Her Mouth
Fine silver, Faux Bone, brass, resin,
polymer, acrylic paint
5" long

Evan Soldinger

Linda Kaye-Moses

LapiCorrugia
Fine silver, sterling,
lapis lazuli

Janise Witt

Jocelyn Cooley

Life Box
Fine silver, cubic zirconia
3" wide by 4" long by 1½" deep

Robert Diamante

Jennifer Kahn

Three Rings
Fine silver, shell, coin, bead
¾" diameter

Marsha Thomas

Lora Hart

Three Beads
Fine silver, 22k gold keum-boo

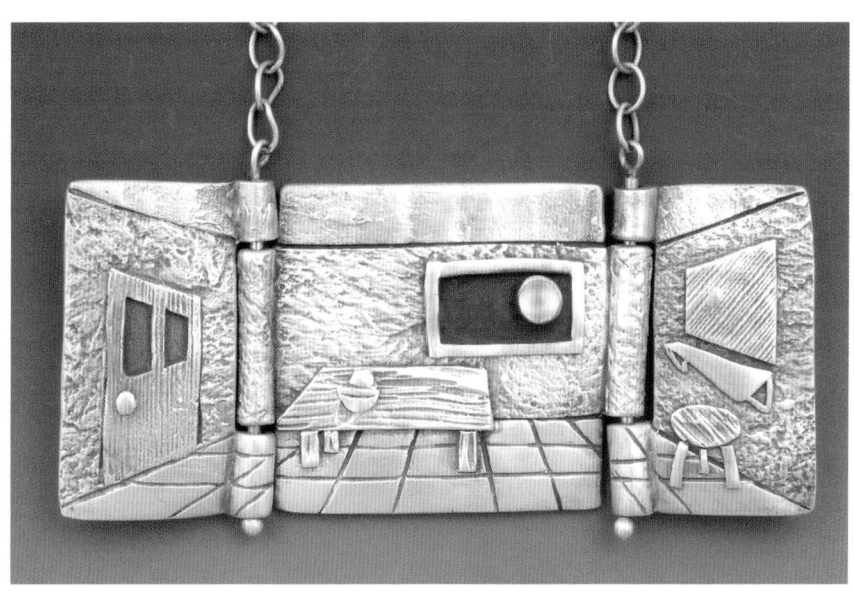

Hadar Jacobson

Hadar Jacobson

Good Night Moon
Fine silver, moonstone
3½" wide

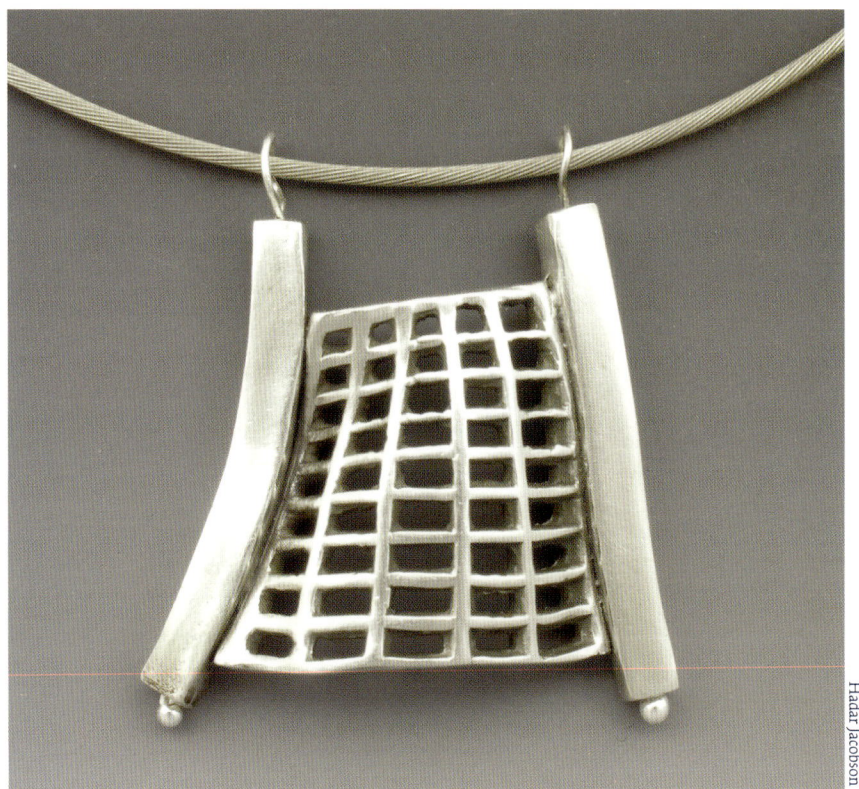

Hadar Jacobson

Laurie Edelman

Screen
Fine silver
1⅝" by 1½"

Courtney Frisse

Wendy Wallin-Malinow

Solar Wind
Fine silver, 24k gold
17" long

RIO GRANDE®

Since 1944

From your friends at

30,000 products, plus all the service and experience that comes with them.

Rio Grande

source code: ADPMC

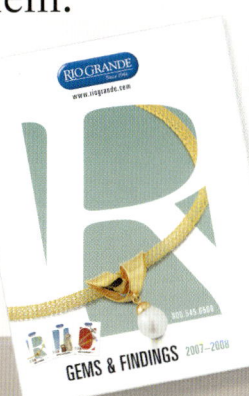

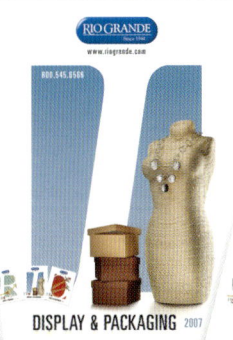

GEMS & FINDINGS 2007–2008

DISPLAY & PACKAGING 2007

TOOLS & EQUIPMENT 2007

phone: 800.545.6566
www.riogrande.com

PMC CONNECTION
CERTIFICATION
PROGRAM

Level 1 - 2 Days, 5 Projects
Learn to use all four forms of PMC - clay, paste/slip, syringe and sheet. Find your true potential with PMC. Learn to include glass, gemstones and organic material as you use the basic PMC techniques to create exciting jewelry designs.

Foldover Pendant with Glass and CZ Linda Bernstein, Playa Vista, CA

Level 2 - 2 Days, 4 Projects
Continue the exploration of PMC with these advanced projects. Set natural gemstones. Create jewelry with sparkling gold and enamel accents.Take your PMC work to the next level of technical excellence.

Bezel Set Natural Stone Mary Ellin D'Agostino, San Pablo, CA

Level 3 - 2 Days, 2 Projects
This is the only Level 3 Certification class available in the US. These projects help the students understand the process and techniques needed to include advanced design elements in complex PMC work.

Hinged Box with Keum Boo and Patina Sherry Fotopoulos, San Antonio, TX

For further information about class schedule and to register visit www.pmcconnection.com or call, toll free, 866-762-2529

- Precious Metal Clay

- Certification, Specialty and Master Classes

- Kilns for PMC, glass and ceramics

- Supplies, tools and equipment

www.PMCConnection.com

8910 Mikuni Avenue • Northridge, CA • 91324
866-PMC-CLAY Toll Free

Everything Metal Clay & More℠

PMCSupply.com is your one stop shop for everything metal clay and much more. We offer everything you could possibly need to create the most amazing metal clay master pieces including build-your-own kits, metal clay, a myriad of kilns, training DVDs, books, stones, findings, chain and a plethora of other metal clay goodies! Visit our website to find everything you need, as well as our gallery of metal clay creations from **Hattie Sanderson, Tim McCreight, Sherri Haab, Shahasp Valentine, Mary Ann Devos, Linda Kline, Jay Humphreys, Renne Lindquist** and many other professional metal clay artists.

✳ **FREE SHIPPING on Retail orders - flat $5.00 on Wholesale orders** ✳

©Renee Lindquist

©Hattie Sanderson

©Sherri Haab

©Renee Lindquist

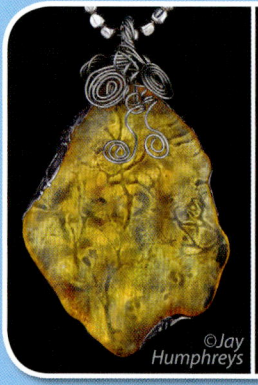
©Jay Humphreys

©Hattie Sanderson

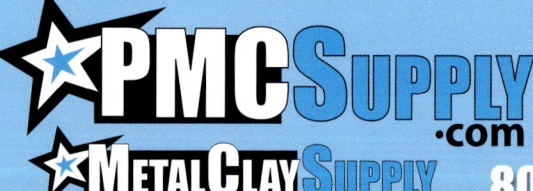

Participating Artists

Participating Artists

PMC GUILD
International

The PMC Guild is a members organization with the mission of providing support, eucation, and exposure for artists working in Precious Metal Clay. Members not only underwrite these important efforts, but have access to special features on our website, such as the ability to promote classes and access the full ten-year archive of the Guild's publications.

The Guild is active around the world, with affiliates and partners in Australia, New Zealand, Great Britain, France, and Japan. Organizers in other countries should contact the Guild for information about these opportunities.

To join the Guild, visit www.PMCguild.com or call toll-free 866-315-6487.

This book is made possible with the support of Mitsubishi Materials, the following companies, and members. Thanks to you all!

CORPORATE SPONSORS

Rio Grande
PMC Connection
PMC Supply
Whole Lotta Whimsy
Metal Clay Findings
Pinzart

SUPPORTING MEMBERS

Lightstone Studio
MED'A Creations
PMC123
Artique
Bisque Imports